BELLS IN WINTER

BELLS IN WINTER

CZESLAW MILOSZ

TRANSLATED BY THE AUTHOR AND LILLIAN VALLEE

THE ECCO PRESS · NEW YORK

First published by The Ecco Press in 1978

18 West 30th Street, New York, N.Y. 10001

Published simultaneously in Canada by

George J. McLeod, Ltd., Toronto

Printed in the United States of America

The Ecco Press logo by Ahmed Yacoubi

Designed by Cynthia Krupat

Grateful acknowledgment is made to the following publications
in which these poems first appeared: American Poetry Review:
"A Felicitous Life," "Bluebeard's Castle," "Calling to Order,"
"Encounter," "How It Was," "Island," "Not This Way,"
"Our Lady of Recovery," "Proof," "Readings," "Study of Loneliness,"
"Temptation," "The Fall," "The View," "The Visitor," "Tidings."
Antaeus: "A Magic Mountain," "Ars Poetica?," "So Little,"
"The Owners," "Vandeans." Some of these poems also
appeared in New Poetry.

Library of Congress Cataloging in Publication Data

Milosz, Czeslaw. / Bells in winter. / I. Title.

PG7158.M553B4 / 891.8'5'17 / 78–5617

ISBN 0-912946-57-1

Third Printing, 1981

CONTENTS

BELLS IN WINTER

ENCOUNTER

We were riding through frozen fields in a wagon at dawn.
A red wing rose in the darkness.

And suddenly a hare ran across the road.
One of us pointed to it with his hand.

That was long ago. Today neither of them is alive,
Not the hare, nor the man who made the gesture.

O my love, where are they, where are they going
The flash of a hand, streak of movement, rustle of pebbles.
I ask not out of sorrow, but in wonder.

1936

A FRIVOLOUS
CONVERSATION

—My past is a stupid butterfly's overseas voyage.
My future is a garden where a cook cuts the throat of a rooster.
What do I have, with all my pain and rebellion?

—Take a moment, just one, and when its fine shell,
Two joined palms, slowly opens
What do you see?

        —A pearl, a second.

—Inside a second, a pearl, in that star saved from time,
What do you see when the wind of mutability ceases?

—The earth, the sky and the sea, richly cargoed ships,
Spring morning full of dew and faraway princedoms.
At marvels displayed in tranquil glory
I look and do not desire for I am content.

1944

TIDINGS

Of earthly civilization, what shall we say?

That it was a system of colored spheres cast in smoked glass,
Where a luminescent liquid thread kept winding and unwinding.

Or that it was an array of sunburst palaces
Shooting up from a dome with massive gates
Behind which walked a monstrosity without a face.

That every day lots were cast, and that whoever drew low
Was marched there as sacrifice: old men, children, young boys and
    young girls.

Or we may say otherwise: that we lived in a golden fleece,
In a rainbow net, in a cloud cocoon
Suspended from the branch of a galactic tree.
And our net was woven from the stuff of signs,
Hieroglyphs for the eye and ear, amorous rings.
A sound reverberated inward, sculpturing our time,
The flicker, flutter, twitter of our language.

For from what could we weave the boundary
Between within and without, light and abyss,
If not from ourselves, our own warm breath,
And lipstick and gauze and muslin,
From the heartbeat whose silence makes the world die?

Or perhaps we'll say nothing of earthly civilization.
For nobody really knows what it was.

—

ISLAND

Think however you like about this island, its ocean whiteness, grottoes overgrown with vines, under violets, springs.

I'm frightened, for I can hardly remember myself there, in one of those medi-terranean civilizations from which one must sail far, through the gloom and rustle of icebergs.

Here a finger points at fields in rows, pear trees, a bridle, the yoke of a water carrier, everything enclosed in crystal, and then I believe that, yes, I once lived there, instructed in those customs and manners.

I pull my coat around me listening to the incoming tide, I rock and lament my foolish ways, but even if I had been wise I would have failed to change my fate.

Lament my foolishness then and later and now, for which I would like so much to be forgiven.

—

HOW IT WAS

Stalking a deer I wandered deep into the mountains and from there I saw.

Or perhaps it was for some other reason that I rose above the setting sun.

Above the hills of blackwood and a slab of ocean and the steps of a glacier, carmine-colored in the dusk.

I saw absence; the mighty power of counter-fulfillment; the penalty of a promise lost for ever.

If, in tepees of plywood, tire shreds and grimy sheet iron, ancient inhabitants of this land shook their rattles, it was all in vain.

No eagle-creator circled in the air from which the thunderbolt of its glory had been cast out.

Protective spirits hid themselves in subterranean beds of bubbling ore, jolting the surface from time to time so that the fabric of freeways was bursting asunder.

God the Father didn't walk about any longer tending the new shoots of a cedar, no longer did man hear his rushing spirit.

His son did not know his sonship and turned his eyes away when passing by a neon cross flat as a movie screen showing a striptease.

This time it was really the end of the Old and the New Testament.

—

7

No one implored, everyone picked up a nodule of agate or diorite to whisper in loneliness: I cannot live any longer.

Bearded messengers in bead necklaces founded clandestine communes in imperial cities and in ports overseas.

But none of them announced the birth of a child-savior.

Soldiers from expeditions sent to punish nations would go disguised and masked to take part in forbidden rites, not looking for any hope.

They inhaled smoke soothing all memory and, rocking from side to side, shared with each other a word of nameless union.

Carved in black wood the Wheel of Eternal Return stood before the tents of wandering monastic orders.

And those who longed for the Kingdom took refuge like me in the mountains to become the last heirs of a dishonored myth.

NOT THIS WAY

Forgive me. I was a schemer like many of those who steal by human habitations at night.

I reckoned the positions of guards before I dared approach closed borders.

Knowing more, I pretended that less would suffice, unlike those who give testimony,

Indifferent to gunfire, hue and cry in the brushwood, and mockery.

Let sages and saints, I thought, bring a gift to the whole Earth, not merely to language.

I protect my good name for language is my measure.

A bucolic, childish language that transforms the sublime into the cordial.

And the hymn or psalm of a choirmaster falls apart, only a canticle remains.

My voice always lacked fullness, I would like to render a different thanksgiving,

And generously, without irony which is the glory of slaves.

Beyond the seven borders, under the morning star.

In the language of fire, water and all the elements.

—

READINGS

You asked me what is the good of reading the Gospels in Greek.
I answer that it is proper that we move our finger
Along letters more enduring than those carved in stone,
And that, slowly pronouncing each syllable,
We discover the true dignity of speech.
Compelled to be attentive we shall think of that epoch
No more distant than yesterday, though the heads of Caesars
On coins are different today. Yet still it is the same eon.
Fear and desire are the same, oil and wine
And bread mean the same. So does the fickleness of the throng
Avid for miracles as in the past. Even mores,
Wedding festivities, drugs, laments for the dead
Only seem to differ. Then, too, for example,
There were plenty of persons whom the text calls
Daimonizomenoi, that is, the demonized
Or, if you prefer, the bedeviled (as for "the possessed"
It's no more than the whim of a dictionary).
Convulsions, foam at the mouth, the gnashing of teeth
Were not considered signs of talent.
The demonized had no access to print and screens,
Rarely engaging in arts and literature.
But the Gospel parable remains in force:
That the spirit mastering them may enter swine,
Which, exasperated by such a sudden clash
Between two natures, theirs and the Luciferic,
Jump into water and drown (which occurs repeatedly).
And thus on every page a persistent reader
Sees twenty centuries as twenty days
In a world which one day will come to its end.

—

STUDY OF LONELINESS

A guardian of long-distance conduits in the desert?
A one-man crew of a fortress in the sand?
Whoever he was. At dawn he saw furrowed mountains
The color of ashes, above the melting darkness,
Saturated with violet, breaking into fluid rouge,
Till they stood, immense, in the orange light.
Day after day. And, before he noticed, year after year.
For whom, he thought, that splendor? For me alone?
Yet it will be here long after I perish.
What is it in the eye of a lizard? Or when seen by a migrant bird?
If I am all mankind, are they themselves without me?
And he knew there was no use crying out, for none of them would save
   him.

—

THE VIEW

The landscape lacked nothing except glorification.
Except royal messengers who would bring their gifts:
A noun with an attribute and an inflected verb.
If only precious oaks would richly shine
When our brave students, on a path over the valley,
Walk and sing "The Ode to Joy."
If at least a solitary shepherd would carve letters in bark.

The landscape lacked nothing except glorification.
But there were no messengers. Thickets, dark ravines,
Forest overhanging forest, a kite wailed.
And who here could manage to institute a phrase?
The view was, who knows, probably pretty.

Far below, all was crumbling: castle halls,
Alleys behind the cathedral, bordellos, shops.
And not a soul. So where could the messengers come from?
After forgotten disasters I was inheriting the earth
Down to the shore of the sea, and above the earth, the sun.

CAESAREA

When we entered the waters of Caesarea
Or were sailing toward it, still straying through atlases,
Gulls were asleep on the smooth sounds between promontories,
A string of ducks flew along the delta in the morning mist.
Phantoms, towers beyond the smoke. A flickering and a sound like metal.
And galleons, of those who had made it to port long before,
Lay rotting at the gates of the city.

How many years were we to learn without understanding.
We roamed about the markets of Caesarea,
We crossed mountain chains and inland seas,
Getting acquainted with a multitude of its peoples and creeds and
      tongues.
Now, when Caesarea is bitterness for us
We are still not sure: were we led astray by the greed of our eyes,
Or did we so firmly believe that it had come true:
Our vocation, our very first calling.

A FELICITOUS LIFE

His old age fell on years of abundant harvest.
There were no earthquakes, droughts or floods.
It seemed as if the turning of the seasons gained in constancy,
Stars waxed strong and the sun increased its might.
Even in remote provinces no war was waged.
Generations grew up friendly to fellow men.
The rational nature of man was not a subject of derision.

It was bitter to say farewell to the earth so renewed.
He was envious and ashamed of his doubt,
Content that his lacerated memory would vanish with him.

Two days after his death a hurricane razed the coasts.
Smoke came from volcanoes inactive for a hundred years.
Lava sprawled over forests, vineyards and towns.
And war began with a battle on the islands.

THE FALL

The death of a man is like the fall of a mighty nation
That had valiant armies, captains and prophets,
And wealthy ports and ships over all the seas,
But now it will not relieve any besieged city,
It will not enter into any alliance,
Because its cities are empty, its population dispersed,
Its land once bringing harvest is overgrown with thistles,
Its mission forgotten, its language lost,
The dialect of a village high upon inaccessible mountains.

———

AN HOUR

Leaves glowing in the sun, zealous hum of bumble bees,
From afar, from somewhere beyond the river, echoes of lingering voices
And the unhurried sounds of a hammer gave joy not only to me.
Before the five senses were opened, and earlier than any beginning
They waited, ready, for all those who would call themselves mortals,
So that they might praise, as I do, life, that is, happiness.

—

TEMPTATION

Under a starry sky I was taking a walk,
On a ridge overlooking neon cities,
With my companion, the spirit of desolation,
Who was running around and sermonizing,
Saying that I was not necessary, for if not I, then someone else
Would be walking here, trying to understand his age.
Had I died long ago nothing would have changed.
The same stars, cities and countries
Would have been seen with other eyes.
The world and its labors would go on as they do.

For Christ's sake, get away from me.
You've tormented me enough, I said.
It's not up to me to judge the calling of men.
And my merits, if any, I won't know anyway.

—

PROOF

And yet you experienced the flames of Hell.
You can even say what they are like: real,
Ending in sharp hooks so that they tear up flesh
Piece by piece, to the bone. You walked in the street
And it was going on: the lashing and bleeding.
You remember, therefore you have no doubt: there is a Hell for certain.

—

AMAZEMENT

O what daybreak in the windows! Cannons salute.
The basket boat of Moses floats down the green Nile.
Standing immobile in the air, we fly over flowers:
Lovely carnations and tulips placed on long low tables.
Heard too are hunting horns exclaiming *hallali*.
Innumerable and boundless substances of the Earth:
Scent of thyme, hue of fir, white frost, dances of cranes.
And everything simultaneous. And probably eternal.
Unseen, unheard, yet it was.
Unexpressed by strings or tongues, yet it will be.
Raspberry ice cream, we melt in the sky.

—

CALLING TO ORDER

You could scream
Because mankind is mad.
But you, of all people, should not.

Out of what thin sand
And mud and slime
Out of what dogged splinters
Did you fashion your castle against the test of the sea,
And now it is touched by a wave.

What chaos
Received bounds, from here to there.
What abyss
Was seen and passed over in silence.
What fear
Of what you are.

It shows itself
But that is not it.
It is named
Yet remains nameless.
It is coming to be
But has not begun.

Your castle will topple
Into the wine-colored
Funereal sea,
She will assuage your pride.

—

Yet you knew how
To use next to nothing.
It is not a matter of wisdom
Or virtue.

So how can you condemn
The unreason of others.

WINDOW

I looked out the window at dawn and saw a young apple tree translucent in brightness.

And when I looked out at dawn once again, an apple tree laden with fruit stood there.

Many years had probably gone by but I remember nothing of what happened in my sleep.

SO LITTLE

I said so little.
Days were short.

Short days.
Short nights.
Short years.

I said so little.
I couldn't keep up.

My heart grew weary
From joy,
Despair,
Ardor,
Hope.

The jaws of Leviathan
Were closing upon me.

Naked, I lay on the shores
Of desert islands.

The white whale of the world
Hauled me down to its pit.

And now I don't know
What in all that was real.

—

A MAGIC MOUNTAIN

I don't remember exactly when Budberg died, it was either two years
  ago or three.
The same with Chen. Whether last year or the one before.
Soon after our arrival, Budberg, gently pensive,
Said that in the beginning it is hard to get accustomed,
For here there is no spring or summer, no winter or fall.

"I kept dreaming of snow and birch forests.
Where so little changes you hardly notice how time goes by.
This is, you will see, a magic mountain."

Budberg: a familiar name in my childhood.
They were prominent in our region,
This Russian family, descendants of German Balts.
I read none of his works, too specialized.
And Chen, I have heard, was an exquisite poet,
Which I must take on faith, for he wrote in Chinese.

Sultry Octobers, cool Julys, trees blossom in February.
Here the nuptial flight of hummingbirds does not forecast spring.
Only the faithful maple sheds its leaves every year.
For no reason, its ancestors simply learned it that way.

I sensed Budberg was right and I rebelled.
So I won't have power, won't save the world?
Fame will pass me by, no tiara, no crown?
Did I then train myself, myself the Unique,
To compose stanzas for gulls and sea haze,
To listen to the foghorns blaring down below?

———

Until it passed. What passed? Life.
Now I am not ashamed of my defeat.
One murky island with its barking seals
Or a parched desert is enough
To make us say: yes, *oui, si.*
"Even asleep we partake in the becoming of the world."
Endurance comes only from enduring.
With a flick of the wrist I fashioned an invisible rope,
And climbed it and it held me.

What a procession! *Quelles délices!*
What caps and hooded gowns!
Most respected Professor Budberg,
Most distinguished Professor Chen,
Wrong Honorable Professor Milosz
Who wrote poems in some unheard-of tongue.
Who will count them anyway. And here sunlight.
So that the flames of their tall candles fade.
And how many generations of hummingbirds keep them company
As they walk on. Across the magic mountain.
And the fog from the ocean is cool, for once again it is July.

———

FROM THE CHRONICLES OF THE TOWN OF PORNIC

Bluebeard's Castle

The castle on the rock briny from surf
Was built in the tenth century. The arrow of a crossbow
Could reach the mast of any ship entering the port at high tide.
The ebb uncovers a thin line of reefs.
As for Gilles de Laval, Baron de Retz,
He was, I think, a hooligan or a teddy boy or a *Halbstarker*.
His father perished when hunting in the year 1415
Because his cutlass missed the tough heart of a boar.
And perhaps Gilles was given too much freedom
Though they taught him how to read and write in Latin
As well as how to appreciate the liberal arts.
In the bad company of his courtly Falstaffs
This pup was the terror of the region.
He was sixteen when he married Catherine de Thouars.
And he was one of the first to come to the aid of Jeanne d'Arc.
Fearless, the right hand of Jeanne,
It was he who supported her, wounded, at the battle of Tournelles.
He grew bored, so he paid poets and actors
And "violated all divine and human rights," says the Chronicle,
Leading a life of debauchery, here, in the castle of Pornic.
He was condemned in Nantes by lay and ecclesiastical courts.
The executioner strangled him but his body did not fall into the flames
Because six women gathered it up to bury it in consecrated ground.
They say that his family, the archbishop and the prince
Put him to death out of greed for his land.

The Owners

La Marquise Brie-Serrant and her daughter Anne
Were arrested for harboring the vicar Galipaud.
They did not lower their eyes when getting into the coach
Because their duty had been done.
On the way to Nantes, more exactly, in Moutiers,
Drunk men punished them for their pride.
A revolutionary tribunal pronounced the verdict
And they did not cry in the death cell.
When they were being led to the place of execution
Bearded strongmen knocked over the sentries.
They were sailors from the corvette "Alcyon"
Anchored in the estuary of the Loire.
Anne, reflecting on the fierceness of the world
Which takes from us the virginity of memory and flesh,
Entered a convent after the death of her mother.
Le Marquis was beheaded in Paris for his part in a plot.
He planned to snatch the King away from the guillotine.
The castle stood empty. Until the poorest of the citizens,
A blacksmith called Misery, settled in it.
Monsieur Lebreton, a merchant, gave him two hundred francs
To get out, and with another twelve hundred
Bought off the debt of fifty thousand left by the previous owners.
The castle was then inherited by Joubert, manufacturer of cloth.

—

Vandeans

O thoughtless Vandeans! That you, regarded as bandits,
Wanted revenge after taking Pornic, is understandable.
And so you shot Viau the tailor, the notary Bonamy, Libau the black-
    smith,
Merchants Martin and Tardiff, the forester Poisson, two shipwrights,
And even old man Naud who was eighty.
But to celebrate the evening of triumph with wine
And to get dead drunk as peasants can
Without even posting some guards?
A detachment led by a priest-patriot is already on its way in the darkness
And you will be slain or taken prisoner.
At dawn holes were dug in the sand on the beach
(Which means that it happened at low tide).
And two hundred fifteen of you were given to the crabs
While two hundred fifty stood there, reeling,
Their mouths dripping with the saliva of terror.
Until recently the testimony of a very old woman
Was repeated here: then, as a child of four,
She was running, basket in hand, along a path near the castle.
Armed men ordered her to leave
Because when prisoners are shot, witnesses are unwelcome.

Our Lady of Recovery

Once there were harsh winters when frost destroyed the vineyards.
Wolves roamed the streets in the darkness.
There were evenings when women arrayed in their finest
Would gather in vain on a cliff to cast spells on the birds.
What the bird sees below is the dark, dark sea.
A rust-colored sail dragged in the furrow of a wave
Looks like algae, the faces of the drowning
Are not those of husbands and lovers.
But century after century Our Lady of Recovery
Extended her arms in a granite chapel.
Indeed, the ocean shows us what we really are:
Children who for a moment feign the wisdom of captains
And humanity is then a beloved family
And a thousand years are counted as one day.
O Holy Mother, save me, my life is so sinful.
Return me to the dear earth, allow me another day.
O Holy Mother, I am not deserving but I will begin anew,
You didn't live far away because You are near me.
And in their dripping hoods, barefoot, with bowed heads
Thinking: why was it me that she saved?
They went to light the promised candle at her altar.
Later they drank, grew boisterous, their women conceived.
Her smile meant that it was all according to her will.

—

ARS POETICA?

I have always aspired to a more spacious form
that would be free from the claims of poetry or prose
and would let us understand each other without exposing
the author or reader to sublime agonies.

In the very essence of poetry there is something indecent:
a thing is brought forth which we didn't know we had in us,
so we blink our eyes, as if a tiger had sprung out
and stood in the light, lashing his tail.

That's why poetry is rightly said to be dictated by a daimonion,
though it's an exaggeration to maintain that he must be an angel.
It's hard to guess where that pride of poets comes from,
when so often they're put to shame by the disclosure of their frailty.

What reasonable man would like to be a city of demons,
who behave as if they were at home, speak in many tongues,
and who, not satisfied with stealing his lips or hand,
work at changing his destiny for their convenience?

It's true that what is morbid is highly valued today,
and so you may think that I am only joking
or that I've devised just one more means
of praising Art with the help of irony.

There was a time when only wise books were read
helping us to bear our pain and misery.
This, after all, is not quite the same
as leafing through a thousand works fresh from psychiatric clinics.

—

And yet the world is different from what it seems to be
and we are other than how we see ourselves in our ravings.
People therefore preserve silent integrity
thus earning the respect of their relatives and neighbors.

The purpose of poetry is to remind us
how difficult it is to remain just one person,
for our house is open, there are no keys in the doors,
and invisible guests come in and out at will.

What I'm saying here is not, I agree, poetry,
as poems should be written rarely and reluctantly,
under unbearable duress and only with the hope
that good spirits, not evil ones, choose us for their instrument.

NOTES

On the need to draw boundaries
Wretched and dishonest was the sea.

Reason to wonder
The ruler of what elements gave us song to praise birth?

According to Heraclitus
The eternally living flame, the measure of all things, just as the measure
of wealth is money.

Landscape
Unbounded forests flowing with the honey of wild bees.

Language
Cosmos, i.e. pain raved in me with a diabolic tongue.

Supplication
From galactic silence protect us.

Just in case
When I curse Fate, it's not me, but the earth in me.

From the store of Pythagorean Principles
Having left your native land, don't look back, the Erinyes are behind
you.

Hypothesis
If, she said, you wrote in Polish to punish yourself for your sins, you will
be saved.

Portrait

He locked himself in a tower, read ancient authors, fed birds on the terrace.

For only in this way could he forget about having to know himself.

Consolation

Calm down. Both your sins and your good deeds will be lost in oblivion.

Do ut des

He felt thankful, so he couldn't not believe in God.

The perfect republic

Right from early morning—the sun has barely made it through the dense maples—they walk contemplating the holy word: Is.

The tempter in the garden

A still-looking branch, both cold and living.

Harmony

Deprived. And why shouldn't you be deprived?
Those better than you were deprived.

Strong or weak point

You were always ready to fall to your knees!
Yes, I was always ready to fall to my knees.

What accompanies us

Mountain stream, footbridge with a rail
remembered down to the smallest burr on its bark.

The West

On straw-yellow hills, over a cold blue sea,
black bushes of thorny oak.

—

33

Inscription to be placed over the unknown grave of L.F.
What was doubt in you, lost, what was faith in you, triumphed.

Epitaph
You who think of us: they lived only in delusion,
Know that we, the People of the Book, will never die.

Memory and memory
Not to know. Not to remember. With this one hope:
That beyond the River Lethe, there is memory, healed.

A God-fearing man
So God heard my request after all, and allowed me to sin in his praise.

On aim in life
O to cover my shame with regal attire!

Medicine
If not for the revulsion at the smell of his skin,
I could think I was a good man.

Longing
Not that I want to be a god or a hero.
Just to change into a tree, grow for ages, not hurt anyone.

Mountains
Wet grass to the knees, in the clearing, raspberry bushes taller than a
man, a cloud on the slope, in the cloud a black forest. And shepherds
in medieval buskins were coming down as we walked up.

In reverse
On the ruins of their homes grows a young forest. Wolves are returning
and a bear sleeps secure in a raspberry thicket.

———

34

Morning

We awoke from a sleep of I don't know how many thousand years.
An eagle flew in the sun again but it didn't mean the same.

Abundant catch (Luke V, 4–10)

On the shore fish toss in the stretched nets of Simon, James and John.
High above, swallows. Wings of butterflies. Cathedrals.

History of the Church

For two thousand years I have been trying to understand what It was.

—

FROM THE RISING
OF THE SUN

1 / The Unveiling

Whatever I hold in my hand, a stylus, reed, quill or a ballpoint,
Wherever I may be, on the tiles of an atrium, in a cloister cell, in a hall
    before the portrait of a king,
I attend to matters I have been charged with in the provinces,
And I begin, though nobody can explain why and wherefore.
Just as I do now, under a dark-blue cloud with a glint of the red horse.
Retainers are busy, I know, in underground chambers,
Rustling rolls of parchment, preparing colored ink and sealing wax.

This time I am frightened. Odious rhythmic speech
Which grooms itself and, of its own accord, moves on.
Even if I wanted to stop it, weak as I am from fever,
Because of a flu like the last one that brought mournful revelations
When, looking at the futility of my ardent years,
I heard a storm from the Pacific beating against the window.
But no, gird up your loins, pretend to be brave to the end
Because of daylight and the neighing of the red horse.

Vast lands. Flickering of hazy trains.
Children walk by an open field, all is gray beyond a Finnish village.
Royza, captain of the cavalry. Mowczan. Angry gales.
Never again will I kneel in my small country, by a river,
So that what is stone in me could be dissolved,
So that nothing would remain but my tears, tears.

———

Chorus:
Hope of old people,
Never assuaged.
They wait for their day
Of power and glory.
For a day of comprehension.
They have so much to accomplish
In a month, in a year,
To the end.

It rolls along, skylike, in the sun on its islands, in the flow of salty
    breezes.
It flies past and does not, new and the same.
Narrowed sculptured boats, a hundred oars, on the stern a dancer
Beats baton against baton, flinging his knees.
Sonorous pagodas, beasts in pearl-studded nets,
Hidden staircases of princesses, floodgates, gardens of lilies.
It rolls along, it flies by, our speech.

Chorus:
He whose life was short can easily be forgiven.
He whose life was long can hardly be forgiven.
When will that shore appear from which at last we see
How all this came to pass and for what reason?

Darkly, darkly cities return.
The roads of a twenty-year-old are littered with maple leaves
As he walks along one acrid morning, looking through the fences at
    gardens
And courtyards, where a black dog barks, and someone chops wood.
Now on a bridge he listens to the babble of the river, bells are resound-
    ing.
Under the pines of sandy bluffs he hears echoes, sees white frost and fog.

—

How did I come to know the scent of smoke, of late autumn dahlias
On the sloping little streets of a wooden town
Since it was so long ago, in a millennium visited in dreams
Far from here, in a light of which I am uncertain?

Was I there, cuddled like a vegetal baby in a seed,
Called long before the hours, one after another, would touch me?
Does so little remain of our labors lasting till evening
That we have nothing left except our completed fate?

Under the dark-blue cloud with a glint of the red horse
I dimly recognize all that has been.
The clothes of my name fall away and disappear.
The stars in wide waters grow smaller.
Again the other, unnamed one, speaks for me.
And he opens fading dreamlike houses
So that I write here in desolation
Beyond the land and sea.

II / Diary of a Naturalist

In search of a four-leaf clover through the meadows at dawn,
In search of a double hazelnut into deep forest.
There we were promised a great, great life
And it waited, though we weren't yet born.

The oak our father, rough was his shoulder.
Sister birch led us with a whisper.
Further and further we went on to meet
The living water in which all strength revives.

Until, wandering through a dense black forest
All the long day of a young summer,
We will come at dusk to the edge of bright waters
Where the king of beavers rules over the crossings.

Fare well, Nature.
Fare well, Nature.

We were flying over a range of snowpeaked mountains
And throwing dice for the soul of the condor.
—Should we grant reprieve to the condor?
—No, we won't grant reprieve to the condor.
It didn't eat from the tree of Knowledge and so it must perish.

In a park by a river a bear blocked our way
And extending his paw begged for assistance.
—Was it this one that frightened lost travelers?

———

—Let's give him a bottle of beer to cheer him up.
Once he had treefuls of honey on his estates.

He loped gracefully across an asphalt freeway
And once more a wood misty with rain moved past in our lights.
—It looked like a cougar.
—That would make sense.
They should be here according to statistics.

Fare well, Nature.
Fare well, Nature.

I show here how my childish dream was denied:

And now, on my school bench but not present, I slip into a picture on a wall in the classroom, "Animals of North America."

Fraternizing with the racoon, stroking the wapiti, chasing wild swans over a caribou trail.

The wilderness protects me, there a gray squirrel can walk for weeks on the treetops.

But I will be called to the blackboard, and who can guess when, in what years.

The chalk breaks in my fingers, I turn around and hear a voice, mine, probably mine:

"White as horse skulls in the desert, black as a trail of interplanetary night

Nakedness, nothing more, a cloudless picture of Motion.

—

40

It was Eros who plaited garlands of fruit and flowers,

Who poured dense gold from a pitcher into sunrises and sunsets.

He and no one else led us into fragrant landscapes

Of branches hanging low by streams, of gentle hills,

And an echo lured us on and on, a cuckoo promised

A place, deep in a thicket, where there is no longing.

Our eyes were touched: instead of decay, the green,

The cinnabar of a tiger lily, the bitter blue of a gentian,

Furriness of bark in half-shade, a marten flickered,

Yes, only delight, Eros. Should we then trust

The alchemy of blood, marry forever the childish earth of illusion?

Or bear a naked light without color, without speech,

That demands nothing from us and calls us nowhere?"

I covered my face with my hands and those sitting on the benches kept silent.

They were unknown to me, for my age was over and my generation lost.

I tell about my acumen at a time when, guessing a few things in advance, I hit upon an idea, certainly not new, but highly regarded by my betters about whom I knew nothing:

—

My generation was lost. Cities too. And nations.
But all this a little later. Meanwhile, in the window, a swallow
Performs its rite of the second. That boy, does he already suspect
That beauty is always elsewhere and always delusive?
Now he sees his homeland. At the time of the second mowing.
Roads winding uphill and down. Pine groves. Lakes.
An overcast sky with one slanting ray.
And everywhere men with scythes, in shirts of unbleached linen
And the dark-blue trousers that were common in the province.
He sees what I see even now. Oh but he was clever,
Attentive, as if things were instantly changed by memory.
Riding in a cart, he looked back to retain as much as possible.
Which means he knew what was needed for some ultimate moment
When he would compose from fragments a world perfect at last.

Everything would be fine if language did not deceive us by finding different names for the same thing in different times and places:

The Alpine shooting star, *Dodecatheon alpinum,*
Grows in the mountain woods over Rogue River,
Which river, in Southern Oregon,
Owing to its rocky, hardly accessible banks,
Is a river of fishermen and hunters. The black bear and the cougar
Are still relatively common on these slopes.
The plant was so named for its pink-purple flowers
Whose slanting tips point to the ground from under the petals,
And resembles a star from nineteenth-century illustrations
That falls, pulling along a thin sheaf of lines.
The name was given to the river by French trappers
When one of them stumbled into an Indian ambush.
From that time on they called it La Rivière des Coquins,
The River of Scoundrels, or Rogue, in translation.

—

I sat by its loud and foamy current
Tossing in pebbles and thinking that the name
Of that flower in the Indian language will never be known,
No more than the native name of their river.
A word should be contained in every single thing
But it is not. So what then of my vocation?

Nonsensical stanzas intrude, about Anusia and *żalia rutéle*, or green rue,
always, it seems, a symbol of life and happiness:

Why did Anusia grow that rue
The evergreen rue in her maiden's garden?
And why did she sing of *żalia rutéle*
So that evening echoes carried over the water?

And where did she go in her wreath of fresh rue?
Did she take the skirt from her coffer when leaving?
And who will know her in the Indian beyond
When her name was Anusia and she is no more?

I give a brief account of what happened to a book which was once our
favorite, *Our Forest and Its Inhabitants*:

The lament of a slaughtered hare fills the forest.
It fills the forest and disturbs nothing there.
For the dying of a particular being is its own private business
And everyone has to cope with it in whatever way he can.
Our Forest and Its Inhabitants. Our, of our village,
Fenced in with a wire. Sucking, munching, digesting,
Growing and being annihilated. A callous mother.
If the wax in our ears could melt, a moth on pine needles,
A beetle half-eaten by a bird, a wounded lizard,
Would all lie at the center of the expanding circles
Of their vibrating agony. That piercing sound

—

Would drown out the loud shots of bursting seeds and buds,
And our child who gathers wild strawberries in a basket.
Would not hear the trilling, nice after all, of the thrush.

I pay homage to Stefan Bagiński who taught me how to operate a microscope and prepare a slide. Nor am I forgetting about the main contributor to my pessimism, and even quote from a work about his deeds in the service of science, published for the use of young people in the year 1890 in Warsaw: Prof. Erazm Majewski, *Doctor Catchfly; Fantastic Adventures in the World of Insects:*

To the masters of our youth, greetings.
To you, my teacher, Mr. Life Science,
Spleeny Bagiński in checkered knickers,
The ruler of *infusoria* and amoebas.
Wherever your skull with its woolly tuft
Reposes, rocked by the whirling elements,
Whatever fate befell your glasses
In their gold-wire rims,
I offer you these words.

And to you, Doctor Catchfly,
Who are free from destruction, the hero
Of a historic expedition to the land of insects.
You live as always on Miodowa in Warsaw
And your servant Gregory dusts carpets every morning,
While you set off on your old bachelor's walk
Through the park, the place of your victory
Over all things subject to ruin and change.

It happened in the summer of the year 187*:

"The day when our naturalist was to lead his beautiful fiancée to the altar was calm, sunny and without a breeze. Precisely the kind of day

—

44

needed for a specimen-gathering expedition. But Dr. Catchfly, already dressed in his frock-coat, was not thinking of two-winged creatures. Attracted by the fine weather and faithful to his habits, he simply decided to spend his last free hour in the Park of the Royal Baths. While walking, he was meditating on the happiness of their future life together when suddenly something flickered before his dreamy eyes: a tiny little two-winged thing. He glanced and stopped, dumbfounded. Before him was a robber fly, but one that he had never seen before! His heart began pounding. He held his breath and drew closer to the leaf in order to better observe this rare specimen. But the wary insect, allowing him just enough time to make sure it was indeed extraordinary, flew off to another branch. Our naturalist, his eyes fixed on the insect, approached on tiptoe but the robber fly, quite smart, it seems, took its leave in time. This was repeated a few times and the frolicsome fly led him to the other side of the flower bed. The naturalist was losing it from sight and finding it again, while time passed. The hour of the wedding arrived but the robber fly placed itself very high, so high, as a matter of fact, that to keep it in sight, it was necessary to climb the tree. There was not a moment to lose."

Ah, subterfuges of Fate! That he was caught
Stalking on a branch, exactly when extending his top hat.
That when hearing this news, the maiden swooned.

She was an unreasonable creature of the fairer sex.
She chose her Earth of tulle and gauze,
Of boudoir mirrors that were easily cracked,
Of faience chamber pots that leave only one ear
To the excavator's shovel. The Earth of midwives, mourners,
Of whispers *Between the Lips and the Cup*,
Or else between lips and a pastry
Devoured in wastelands by posthumous descendants.
An ordinary Earth, after all. Priceless for many.
O may the earth lie lightly on her, though light it is never.

—

If not for that day, admit it, John Catchfly,
Your zeal would have grown tame among lampshades.
A passion, pure and manifest,
Would not have led you to your destiny,
Until at dawn on a meadow in the Tatra mountains,
In the Valley of White Water and Rówienka,
Looking at the red of the rising sun,
Obedient to the formula, you drank the elixir
And went down to where there is neither guilt nor complaint.

Tiny, I wandered with you in the unfathomed land
Beneath stalks of grass as thick as cedars,
In the din and blast of diaphanous, winged machines.
I would stand in the middle of a rugged leaf
And, over the gloom of a swampy chasm
I pulled myself along a strand of gossamer.

You wrote down: "horrible conditions."
In sap, mush, glue, millions and millions
Of entangled legs, wings and abdomens
Struggle to free themselves, weaken, stiffen forever.
The fat flesh of caterpillars being devoured alive
By the rapacious progeny of inquisitive flies,
Undulates its segments, and grazes unconcerned.
O humanitarian from the age of debates,
What sort of scientist are you, why do you feel compassion?
Is it proper to suddenly get incensed
When on a black, smoldering plain
You arrive at the gates of a burned-down city,
Witness and judge in a hall of dead ants?

You infected me with your pity for computers
Dressed in chitin cloaks, in transparent armor.
And in my child's imagination

—

I still bear your mark, O philosopher of pain.
But I don't hold a grudge, Dr. *honoris causa*
Of Heidelberg and Jena. I am glad
That the white of the ivory on your cane still shines
As if it has never been dimmed by fire
And someone still rode in carriages down the avenues.

I try to describe concisely what I experienced when instead of choosing
the profession of a traveler-naturalist I turned toward other goals:

That's probably why I went on a pilgrimage.
The direction those will recognize who, for instance,
Having visited the caves near Les Eyzies,
Stopping perhaps at noon in Sarlat,
From there took the road that leads to Souillac
Where a bas-relief in a Romanesque portal
Tells the adventures of Monk Theophilus
From Adana in Cilicia, and where the prophet Isaiah
For eight centuries has persisted in a violent gesture
As if he were plucking the strings of an invisible harp.
And on and on, into winding dells, until suddenly
It appears high, so high, that jewel of wayfarers,
As desired as a nest in the top of a fir tree
Was in our boyhood: Roc Amadour.
But I'm not insistent. A road to Compostela
Or to Jasna Góra would instruct you as well.
Pursuing and passing by. Here a mossy rock
Runs, becomes more distinct at every curve,
Then fades in the distance. There, a river flashes
Beyond the trees and the arc of a bridge. But, remember,
Neither the view will stop us, nor the kingfisher
Stitching together the two banks with the bright thread of its flight,
Nor the maiden in the tower, though she lures us with a smile
And blindfolds us before she leads us to her chamber.

———

I was a patient pilgrim. And so I notched
Each month and year on my stick, since it neared me to my aim.
Yet when at last I arrived after many years
What happened there, many would know, I think,
Who in the parking lot at Roc Amadour
Found a space and then counted the steps
To the upper chapel, to make sure that this was it:
Because a wooden Madonna with a child in a crown
Was surrounded by a throng of impassive art lovers.
As I did. Not a step further. Mountains and valleys
Crossed. Through flames. Wide waters. And unfaithful memory.
The same passion but I hear no call.
And the holy had its abode only in denial.

—

JJJ / Over Cities

1

If I am responsible
It is not for everything.
I didn't support the theses of Copernicus.
I was neither for nor against in Galileo's case.
My ships have never left the pond to sail the seas.
When I was born, locomotives ran on rails
Moving in a jumble of wheels and pistons,
And the echo of an express train rang wide
Through forests no longer primeval.
The district was inhabited by folk, Jews and gentlemen.
You went by horse cart to buy kerosene, herring and salt,
But in the towns they were using electricity.
It was said that someone had invented the wireless telegraph.
Books were already written. Ideas thoroughly discussed.
The ax was put to the tree.

2

"He that leadeth into captivity, shall go into captivity": thus began my
age on the planet Earth. Later on I became a teacher in a city by a
great sea and I had just turned away from the blackboard on which they
could read, scribbled in my crooked writing: "Maximus the Confessor"
and the dates "580–662." A multitude of their faces before me, these
boys and girls, born when I was composing the first stanza of a threnody
to be read at a memorial service, grew up before I managed to finish
the poem. Then, putting aside my chalk, I addressed them in the fol-
lowing words:

"Yes, it is undeniable that extraordinary fates befell our species, pre-cisely those from which Maximus the Confessor wanted to protect us, suspecting as he did the devilish temptation in the truth of reason. Yet while we hear everyone advising us to understand clearly causes and ef-fects, let us beware of those perfectly logical though somewhat too eager arguments. Certainly, it is distressing not to know where this force that carries us away comes from or where it leads. But let us observe restraint and limit ourselves to statements which in our intention will be state-ments and nothing else. Let us formulate it thus: yes, the Universal is devouring the Particular, our fingers are heavy with Chinese and Assyrian rings, civilizations are as short-lived as weeks of our lives, places which not long ago were celebrated as homelands under oak trees are now no more than states on a map, and each day we ourselves lose letter after letter from our names which still distinguish us from each other."

3

Once upon a time they inhabited the land. The high and low sun di-
    vided their year.
In fog and mist after St. Michael's, when the angel announces to the
    seed,
Through the four Sundays of Advent and Ember days
Until the blind, the lame and the crippled rejoice, the power trembles,
The sages of the world trudge through the snow protecting myrrh,
    frankincense and gold.
Frost makes the trees crack in the woods, candles are brought home on
    Candlemas,
He wanders by Genezaret, time for their bearish dances.
The double-bass and the drum at Shrovetide until Ash Wednesday.
And lo our little sun / / warms the frozen earth again
Riding past green corn / / palm in hand / / the King enters Jerusalem.

4

It is a ship in the likeness of a trireme or an Egyptian sailboat.

—

In any case the same as in the days when gods used to call from island to island, their hands cupped to their mouths.

Driven by a small motor, it comes near on a Pacific swell.

And in the rustle of the surf, runs aground high on the beach.

They are running, a crowd of them. On the deck, on the mast, their motley nakedness.

Until the whole ship is covered with a swarm opening and closing its wings,

With men and women from the end of the twentieth century.

Waking up I understood the meaning or, rather, I almost did.

5

A life unendurable but it was endured.
Cattle being driven to pasture in early spring. Speech betrays me here:
I don't know what to call a strip of land fenced with poles
That leads from the last huts of the village up to the forest.
(I have always lacked words and have not been a poet
If a poet is supposed to take pleasure in words.)
So, here is the eldest shepherd and his bags,
And his cross-gartered legs and the longest whipstock.
Two striplings with him. One is carrying a birch-bark trumpet,
The other an old-fashioned pistol, its barrel fixed with a string.
Really seen. Near Širvintai or Grinkiškai.
Long before I entered the monastery,
The light over an always radiant sandstone column,
The same today as in the time of Frankonian kings,
Because I wanted to earn a day of comprehension,

—

Or even a single second, when those three
Would also reveal themselves, each in his unique essence.

6

I was long in learning to speak, now I let days pass without a word.

Incessantly astonished by the day of my birth, once only from the beginning to the end of time.

Born of a foolhardy woman with whom I am united, and whom I, an old man, pity in my dreams.

Her funny dresses, her dances, so utterly lost yet so close again.

And to call her a different name than years ago, childishly unique.

Means to gauge, forget, number myself as well.

O what happened and when to *principium individuationis?*

Where is the calamus by the river with its scent, mine alone, and for no one else?

Through what meadows burnt brown does she run with me in her arms

Carrying me to safety, away from the teeth of a beast?

My memory is shut, I don't know who I really was.

Have I fulfilled anything, have I been of use to anyone?

And she, who offered me to Our Lady of Ostrabrama,

How and why was she granted what she asked for in her prayer?

—

A handless performer with his collection of butterflies,

A fisherman by a lack, proud of his nets, the best in the county,

A gardener growing plants from beyond the seas.

Everything taken away. Crossed out. All our treasures.

So that we are alone at the trial in the dark

And hear her steps nearby, and think she has forgiven.

7

Sir Hieronymus took me by the arm and led me to the park
Where, at the turn of the lane, before a moss-covered Ceres,
A view opened upon meadows, the river and the whole valley
Up to the towers of a church in the town beyond the forest.
And he was snapping his snuffbox and unhurriedly telling
Of his adventures in St. Petersburg or Naples,
Wittily describing the various countries.
He dealt at length with the swamps of Polésine
Which he once crossed on his way to Ravenna
From Venice, and argued that Jesuits from that province
Named similar Lithuanian swamps: Polesia.
Then he reminisced about Count de Saint Germain
Or about the lost Book of Hieroglyphic Figures.
Just then the sun was setting over our land.
And he had hardly put his handkerchief into his pocket
When the birds began to sing as in early morning
And the full light of daybreak burst into noon.
Quicker and quicker. A century in half an hour.
And where is Sir Hieronymus? Where did I go? Here there is no one.

—

IV / A Short Recess

1

Life was impossible, but it was endured.
Whose life? Mine, but what does that mean?

During recess, biting into a sandwich wrapped in paper
I stand under the wall in chubby meditation.

And I would have been someone I have never been.
And I would have obtained what I have never obtained.
Jackdaws beyond the window would have been remembered
By another I, not the one in whose words I am thinking now.

And if they say that all I heard was the rushing of a Heraclitean river
That will be enough, for the mere listening to it wore me down.
Scribes in dim rooms calculated on their abacuses.
Or perhaps men drove herds amid the smoke of distant fires.
Abandoned clothes kept for a moment the shape of arms and shoulders.
Pine needles fell onto a plush teddy bear.
And already new peoples with their numerous carts and a cannon.
What else could I be concerned with in Ostrogothic camps?

If only my early love had come true.
If only I had been happy walking down Harbor Street
(which, anyway, did not lead to a harbor
But only to wet logs beyond the sawmills).
Had I been counted among the elders of our city,

—

And traveled abroad on an assignment.
Had we concluded an alliance with Ferrara.

Whoever is born just once on earth
Could have been that man whom Isis visited in a dream
And have gone through an initiation
To say afterwards: I saw.
I saw the radiant sun at midnight.
I trod Proserpina's threshold.
I passed through all the elements and returned.
I came into the presence of the gods below and the gods above
And adored them face to face.

Or a gladiator, a slave
Under an inscription on a level stone:
"i was not, i was, i am not, i do not desire."*

2
—Most distinguished voyager, from where do you hail?

—My city, in a valley among wooded hills
Under a fortified castle at the meeting of two rivers,
Was famous for its ornate temples:
Churches, Catholic and Orthodox, synagogues and mosques.
Our country cultivated rye and flax, it rafted timber as well.
Our army was composed of a lancer regiment,
Dragoons and a regiment of Tartar horsemen.
The postal stamps of our state
Represented phantasms
Sculpted long ago by two artists,
Friends or enemies, Pietro and Giovanni.
Our schools taught dogmatics,

* non fui, fui, non sum, non desidero.

—

55

Apologetics, sentences from the Talmud and Titus Livius.
Aristotle was highly regarded,
Though not as highly as sack races and jumping over fires
On Saint John's Eve.

—Most distinguished voyager, what was your eon like?

—Comic. Terror is forgotten.
Only the ridiculous is remembered by posterity.
Death from a wound, from a noose, from starvation
Is one death, but folly is uncounted and new every year.
I took part, I tied neckties
For no purpose and danced dances for no purpose.
A customer, a buyer of sweaters and pomade,
A mimicker, a shy guest,
A fop impressed by his reflection in shop windows.
I was overgrown by the bark of unconsciousness.
I tried hard to imagine another earth and could not.
I tried hard to imagine another heaven and could not.

3

There is an understanding and a covenant
Between all those whom time has defeated and released.
They tap their hammers, put curl paper in their hair,
Walk crooked sidewalks on urgent errands.
Cripples, harlots, swindlers, potentates.
And the duration of their city has no end,
Though they will no longer buy or sell
Nor take for themselves a husband or wife,
In mirrors they are not visible to themselves, or to anyone.
Their linen, wool, calico and sateen
Sent back to them, as it should be, a little later,
Roll up and shimmer and gently rustle
Under the immovable light of street lamps or sun.

—

Forgiving each other and forgiven,
My fellow messengers, a taciturn retinue,
Though they never stop busying themselves in their streets and market-
    places,
Simultaneously (as we are wont to say) here and there.

4

I wanted glory, fame and power.
But not just in one city of modest renown.
So I fled to countries whose capitals
Had boulevards lustrous beneath incandescent lamps
And, here and there, the outlines of Ionian columns.
I did not learn to value the honors one received there.
A sandy plain showed through every form.
So I ran further, to the center of Megalopolis
In the belief that there was a center, though there was none.
I would have wept over my exposed delusion
Had the custom of regretting our offenses been preserved.
At best I would prostrate myself
And turn to my silent retinue:
Tell me, why should it be me, why exactly me?
Where are the others whose love was real and strong?
Should he remain faithful who didn't want to be faithful?

5

I made a pledge, what kind, I don't remember.
I wore a silver scout badge, then a gold one.
I took an oath, in mystical lodges, in underground assemblies
Swearing by the freedom of the people, or perhaps by brotherhood.
I wasn't to be obedient to my slogans or my chiefs.
Some lazy earthly spirits from under the roots of trees
Had obviously made other arrangements
Having a little laugh at the expense of my morals.
Engaged in weighty discussion on killing for the common good

My clear-eyed companions glanced distractedly
As I passed their table, a naive lute player.
And while they sat at their chess games (the winner was to execute the
    verdict)
I believed they were taking part in the tournaments for fun.
How I envied them: so magnificent,
So free from what I guarded as my shameful secret:
That, like the mermaid from Andersen's tale
I tried to walk correctly but a thin pain
Reminded me that I was foolish to try to imitate people.

6

And there was a holiday in Megalopolis.
Streets were closed to traffic, people walked in a procession.
The statue of a god slowly moved along:
A phallus four stories high
Surrounded by a crowd of priests and priestesses
Who tossed about in a whirling dance.
A service was also being celebrated in Christian churches
Where the liturgy consisted of discussion
Under the guidance of a priest in Easter vestment
On whether we should believe in life after death,
Which the president then put to the vote.
So I betook myself to an evening party
In a glass house at the edge of a mountain,
Where, silent, they stood observing a landscape of the planet:
A sparkling plain of metal or salt,
Absinthe lands furrowed by erosions,
White observatories far away on the summit.
The sun was setting in cardinal crimson.

After shootings and bitterness and songs and lamentations
It is not I who is going to tear at bandages and break seals.

—

What if I was merely an ignorant child
And served the voices that spoke through me?

Who can tell what purpose is served by destinies
And whether to have lived on earth means little
Or much.

V / The Accuser

You say a name, but it's not known to anyone.

Either because that man died or because
He was a celebrity on the banks of another river.

Chiaromonte
Miomandre
Petöfi
Mickiewicz

Young generations are not interested in what happened
Somewhere else, long ago.

And what about your teachers who repeated:
Ars longa, vita brevis?

Their laurel-crowned deceptions will soon be over.

Do you still say to yourself: *non omnis moriar?*

O yes, not all of me shall die, there will remain
An item in the fourteenth volume of an encyclopedia
Next to a hundred Millers and Mickey Mouse.

A traveler. Far away. And a low sun.
You sit in a ditch and to your bearded mouth
You raise a slice of bread cut off with a penknife.

—

And there, splendor. Parades. Carriages. Youth all in flowers.
A short while ago you were one of them. Now you are watching.
Your sons ride there and do not know you.

You don't like this subject. Fine. Let's change it then.
What about those medieval dialogues before daybreak.
My most gracious and honorable body,
I, your soul, you declaim, I command you:
It's time to get up, check the date.
There are many tasks to be done today.
Serve me a little longer, just a bit.
I don't know what is going on in your dark tunnels,
At what moment you'll deny and overthrow me,
On what day your cosmos will congeal and collapse.

And you hear in reply: a bone cracks,
Murky blood grumbles, accelerates its rhythm,
Pain answers close in sign language,
A megalithic gurgle, whisper, indictments.

Confess, you have hated your body,
Loving it with unrequited love. It has not fulfilled
Your high expectations. As if you were chained to
Some little animal in perpetual unrest,
Or worse, to a madman, and a Slavic one at that.

What beauty. What light. An echo.
You lean from the window of a train, behind the house of the signalman
Children wave their kerchiefs. Woods flow by. An echo.
Or she, in a long dress embroidered in gold
Steps down and down the stairs, your beloved.

The so-called sights of the earth. But not many.
You started on a journey and are not sated.

—

Spring dances go on but there is no dancer.
In truth, perhaps you never took part in all that.
A spirit pure and scornfully indifferent,
You wanted to see, to taste, to feel and nothing more.
For no human purpose. You were a passer-by
Who makes use of hands and legs and eyes
As an astrophysicist uses shiny screens,
Aware that what he perceives has long since perished.
"Sweet and faithful animals." How is one to live with them
If they run and strive, while those things are no more?

Do you remember your textbook of Church History?
Even the color of the page, the scent of the corridors.
Indeed, quite early you were a gnostic, a Marcionite,
A secret taster of Manichean poisons.
From our bright homeland cast down to the earth,
Prisoners delivered to the ruin of our flesh
Unto the Archon of Darkness. His is the house and law.
And this dove, here, over Bouffalowa Street
Is his as you yourself are. Descend, fire.
A flash—and the fabric of the world is undone.

This sin and guilt. And to whom should you complain?
I know your microscopes, your many labors,
And your secrets and your life spent
In the service of self-will, not out of self-will.

One summer day, one summer day.
A little armchair adorned with a garland of peonies and jasmine.
Your short legs dangle. All applaud.
A choir of peasants sings a song.

Until you reach the crossroads. There will be two paths.
One difficult and down, another easy and up.

———

Take the difficult one, simple Johnny. Again two paths.
One difficult and up, another easy and down.
Go up and it will lead you to the castle.

The road weaves upward accompanied by a drum and a flute,
Round and round the bends, where the scent is more and more honeyed.
Plaited beehives, their straw shines like brass,
Sunflowers in rows, thyme.
And there, four turrets: facing East, West, North and South.
Where you enter the gate it's as if they were waiting for you.
Complete silence in a rose garden,
Around it, an expanse of green hills,
Of blue-green, up to the very clouds.

A pebble grates on the path. And presto! you fly as in dreams.
Black and white griffins on marble floors,
Parquetry of dim rooms. Yes, you were expected.
You don't have to say who you are. Everyone here knows and loves you.
Eyes meeting eyes, hands touching hands. What communion.
What timeless music of saved generations.

And whoever that man is, from Provence, judging by his dress,
His words, when he addresses beautiful ladies, old men and youths,
Are yours as well, as if he and you had long been one:
"Behold the sword that separates Tristan and Iseult.
Revealed to us was the contradiction between life and truth.
In the forgetting of earthly years is our movement and peace.
In our prayer for the last day is our consolation."

There was no castle. You were simply listening to a record.
A needle, swaying lightly on a black frozen pond,
Led the voices of dead poets out into the sun.
Then you thought in disgust:

—

Bestiality
Bestialité
Bestialità

Who will free me
From everything that my age will bequeath?
From infinity plus. From infinity minus.
From a void lifting itself up to the stars?

Throats.
Choking.
Fingers sinking.
Into flesh.
Which in an instant will cease to live.
A naked heap.
Quivering.
Without sound.
Behind thick glass.

And what if that was you, that observer behind thick glass?

Well, it happened long ago, in Ecbatana.
In Edessa, if you prefer. Be it as it may, a chronicle
In which nothing is certain and no evidence
Against any of you. Or against you alone.

You all rushed to arrange your households.
To smash tablets. Cart them away. Blood
Was washed from the walls with soap, sand and chlorine.

In a barber's chair somewhere in a Southern city.
Summer heat, jingling, a tambourine.
And a pythoness on the sidewalk
Rocks her swarthy belly in a ring of onlookers.

—

While here they trim your gray hair and sideburns
O Emperor.
Franz Josef.
Nicholas.
Ego.

—Yet I have learned how to live with my grief.

—As if putting words together has been of help.

—Not true, there were others, grace and beauty,
I bowed to them, revered them,
I brought them my gifts.

—And all you do is repeat:
If only there were enough time.
If only there were enough time.

You would like to lead a gathering of people
To a ritual of purification through the columns of a temple.

A ritual of purification? Where? When? For whom?

———

VI / Bells in Winter

Once, when returning from far Transylvania
Through mountain forests, rocks and Carpathian ridges,
Halting by a ford at the close of day
(My companions had sent me ahead to look
For passage), I let my horse graze
And out of the saddlebag took the Holy Scripture;
The light was so gracious, murmur of streams so sweet,
That reading Paul's epistles, and seeing the first star,
I was soon lulled into a profound sleep.

A young man in ornate Greek raiment
Touched my arm and I heard his voice:
"Your time, O mortals, hastens by like water,
I have descended and known its abyss.
It was I, whom cruel Paul chastised in Corinth
For having stolen my father's wife,
And by his order I was to be excluded
From the table at which we shared our meals.
Since then I have not been in gatherings of the saints,
And for many years I was led by the sinful love
Of a poor plaything given to temptation,
And so we doomed ourselves to eternal ruin.
But my Lord and my God, whom I knew not,
Tore me from the ashes with his lightning,
In his eyes your truths count for nothing,
His mercy saves all living flesh."

—

Awake under a huge starry sky,
Having received help unhoped for,
Absolved of care about our paltry life,
I wiped my eyes wet with tears.

No, I have never been to Transylvania.
I have never brought messages from there to my church.
But I could have.
This is an exercise in style.
The pluperfect tense
Of countries imperfective.

But what I am going to tell you now is not invented.
The narrow street, just opposite the university
Was called, in fact, Literary Lane.
On the corner, a bookstore; but not books, just sheaves of paper
Up to the very ceiling. Unbound, tied with string,
Print and handwriting, in Latin, Cyrillic script,
In Hebrew letters. From a hundred, three hundred years ago.
Now it seems to me like quite a fortune.
From this bookstore you could see a similar one
Facing it. And their owners
Were similar, too: faded beards
Long black caftans, red eyelids.
They hadn't changed since the day Napoleon passed through the town.
Nothing has changed here. The privilege of stones?
They always are, for that is the way they like it. Beyond the second store
You turn along a wall and pass a house
Where a poet, famous in our city,
Wrote a tale about a princess named Grażyna.
Next, a wooden gate studded with nails
As huge as fists. Under the vault, to the right,
Stairs smelling of oil paint, where I live.

—

Not that I myself chose Literary Lane.
It just happened, there was a room for rent,
Low-ceilinged, with a bay window, an oak bed,
Heated well that severe winter by a stove
That used to devour logs brought from the hallway
By the old servant woman, Lisabeth.

There is, it would seem, no reason
(For I have departed to a land more distant
Than one that can be reached by roads leading through woods and
    mountains)
To bring that room back here.

Yet I belong to those who believe in *apokatastasis*.
That word promises reverse movement,
Not the one that was set in *katastasis*,
And appears in the Acts, 3, 21.

It means: restoration. So believed: St. Gregory of Nyssa,
Johannes Scotus Erigena, Ruysbroeck and William Blake.

For me, therefore, everything has a double existence.
Both in time and when time shall be no more.

And so, one morning. In biting frost,
All is cold and gray. And in that sleepy haze
A span of air suffused with carmine light.
Banks of snow, roadways made slippery by sleighs
Grow rosy. As do wisps of smoke, puffs of vapor.
Bells jingle nearby, then farther away, shaggy horses
Covered with hoarfrost, every hair distinct.
And then the pealing of bells. At Saint John's
And the Bernardines', at Saint Casimir's
And the Cathedral, at the Missionaries'

—

And Saint George's, at the Dominicans'
And Saint Nicholas', at Saint Jacob's.
Many many bells. As if the hands pulling the ropes
Were building a huge edifice over the city.

So that Lisabeth wrapped up in her cape could go to morning mass.

I have thought for a long time about Lisabeth's life.
I could count the years. But I prefer not to.
What are years, if I see the snow and her shoes
Funny, pointed, buttoned on the side,
And I am the same, though the pride of the flesh
Has its beginning and its end.

Pudgy angels are blowing their trumpets again.
And him, the stooped priest in his chasuble
I would compare today to a scarab
From the Egyptian division of the Louvre.
Our sister Lisabeth in the communion of saints—
Of witches ducked and broken on the wheel
Under the image of the cloud-enfolded Trinity
Until they confess that they turn into magpies at night;
Of wenches used for their masters' pleasure;
Of wives who received a letter of divorce;
Of mothers with a package under a prison wall—
Follows the letters with her black fingernail,
When the choirmaster, a sacrificer, a Levite
Ascending the stairs, sings: *Introibo ad altare Dei.*
Ad Deum qui laetificat juventutem meam.

Prie Dievo kurs linksmina mano jaunystė.

Mano jaunystė.
My youth.

—

69

As long as I perform the rite
And sway the censer and the smoke of my words
Rises here.

As long as I intone:
Memento etiam, Domine, famulorum famularumque tuarum
Qui nos praecesserunt.

Kurie pirma musu nuèjo.

What year is this? It's easy to remember.
This is the year when eucalyptus forests froze in our hills
And everyone could provide himself with free wood for his fireplace
In preparation for the rains and storms from the sea.

In the morning we were cutting logs with a chain saw.
And it is a strong, fierce dwarf, crackling and rushing in the smell of
      combustion.
Below, the bay, the playful sun,
And the towers of San Francisco seen through rusty fog.

And always the same consciousness unwilling to forgive.

Perhaps only my reverence will save me.

If not for it, I wouldn't dare pronounce the words of prophets:

"Whatever can be Created can be Annihilated; Forms cannot;
The Oak is cut down by the Ax, the Lamb falls by the Knife,
But their Forms Eternal Exist forever. Amen. Hallelujah!

"For God himself enters Death's Door always with those that enter
And lies down in the Grave with them, in Visions of Eternity

—

70

Till they awake and see Jesus and the Linen Clothes lying
That the Females had woven for them and the Gates of their Father's
    House."

And if the city, there below, was consumed by fire
Together with the cities of all the continents,
I would not say with my mouth of ashes that it was unjust.
For we lived under the Judgment, unaware.

Which Judgment began in the year one thousand seven hundred fifty-
    seven,

Though not for certain, perhaps in some other year.
It shall come to completion in the sixth millennium, or next Tuesday.
The demiurge's workshop will suddenly be stilled. Unimaginable silence.
And the form of every single grain will be restored in glory.
I was judged for my despair because I was unable to understand this.

Czeslaw Milosz, Polish poet, essayist, and novelist, was born in Lithuania in 1911. He was one of the leaders of the avant-garde poetry movement in Poland in the 1930s, was in the Resistance during World War II, and edited an anti-Nazi anthology, *Invincible Song*. After several years in the diplomatic service he severed his ties with the postwar Polish government and came to America. He now teaches in the Department of Slavic Languages and Literatures at the University of California, Berkeley. Professor Milosz was awarded the 1978 Neustadt International Prize for Literature.